Original title:
Feathers and Fortune

Copyright © 2025 Creative Arts Management OÜ
All rights reserved.

Author: Rosalie Bradford
ISBN HARDBACK: 978-1-80586-180-5
ISBN PAPERBACK: 978-1-80586-652-7

Celestial Down

In a world where birds wear hats,
They gossip and discuss their spats.
A squirrel steals a wedding cake,
While pigeons plan a grand mistake.

A dapper crow with shades to match,
Teaches ducks to tango and catch.
The sparrows throw a wild parade,
With twirling moves that never fade.

The Serpent's Embrace

A snake in shades and polka dots,
Sips tea while tying up the knots.
He slinks and slides, all debonair,
And hisses jokes that fill the air.

His friends, a crew of silly birds,
They chirp and laugh, forget their words.
In a garden where the mischief brews,
You'll find trouble with a side of blues.

Plumage of Destiny

A peacock jumped into the fray,
Proclaiming, "I was born this way!"
With glittering feathers, he takes flight,
But lands face-first, oh what a sight!

The robin chuckles, what a show!
As the sparrows join, they steal the glow.
They sport the most bizarre attire,
Dancing wildly, never tire.

The Dappled Dream

A raccoon dreams of disco lights,
Wearing sparkles that shine so bright.
He twirls with glee beneath the moon,
While butterflies join in the tune.

The night is filled with silly prance,
Each critter joins the fun romance.
In a world that turns topsy-turvy,
They laugh, they chase, so sweetly swervy.

Kindred Spirits in the Clouds

In the sky, a bird made a fuss,
Chasing its dreams, but lost on the bus.
With a wink and a flap, it borrowed a ride,
And laughed as it soared on a whimsy tide.

Cloud pals waved hello, what a sight!
In a game of tag, they danced with delight.
One tried to dive, only to glide,
Splat on a raindrop, what a misguide!

The Artistry of Flight and Fancy

A seagull donned shades, all cool and bright,
Performing a ballet high in the light.
With a twist and a spin, it drew all the eyes,
Landing in ketchup, what a surprise!

A pigeon tried breakdancing, oh what a scene,
But tripped on a crumb and turned quite mean.
Yet laughter erupted, all feathers aside,
Who knew that mishaps could cause such pride!

Silver Linings in Soaring

Up in the air, where the whimsies play,
A robin wears bling for a bright display.
It shimmered and sparkled, then lost its bling,
And started a search like it's hunting for spring.

As it looped and swooped, oh, what a crack!
Finding its treasure stuck to a snack.
With a chuckle and cheer, it donned its new find,
Saying, "It's a crown! I'm the king of mankind!"

An Odyssey of Lucky Plumes

A vulture with visions of riches and gold,
Planned a grand quest that was bold and uncontrolled.
It searched every canyon, each nook and glade,
Only to find it was just a charade.

Off in the distance, a peacock preened,
Accidentally twirling, and narrowly gleaned.
With a snap and a clap, it stole the show,
And became a fortune, the star of the glow!

The Splendor of Silent Success

In a nest of dreams we lay,
The early worm won't get today.
With a wink and a cheerful grin,
Who needs to hurry? Let's begin!

A squirrel had a grand old scheme,
To gather acorns, so it seemed.
But when he tried to climb a tree,
He slipped and landed next to me!

Opportunities on a Wing

A bird flew by with shiny shoes,
Chasing worms, he heard the muse.
He danced and twirled on a nearby wire,
While the pigeons laughed, 'What a flyer!'

His luck was light, like the clouds above,
He'd strut and peck, quite the dove.
But when he found a shiny coin,
He dropped it quick, oh what a join!

Hand in Hand with Hopes

Two pigeons perched with dreams in tow,
Planning heists for crumbs below.
They plotted snacks and tasty treats,
While humans walked, they'd steal their eats!

A friendly crow joined in their goals,
With laughter ringing from their souls.
But when they spotted a giant pie,
They dove too fast—oh my, oh my!

Aerial Echoes of Abundance

A seagull squawked at morning light,
'Come, join me in this captivating flight!'
With a trail of chips left in the breeze,
He led his crew with jokes and tease.

Above the beach, they swooped and swirled,
A feathery frenzy all unfurled.
Yet when they tripped on a bathers' hat,
They laughed and rolled like silly brats!

The Texture of Triumph

A bird once wore a shiny hat,
It thought it wise, but just a cat.
With every flap, it lost its style,
Chasing dreams, it tripped awhile.

Now it struts with feathers bold,
But tales of glory? Just retold.
For every win, a funny twist,
That silly bird can't help but tryst.

The Voyage of the Vagabond's Dream

A wanderer on a ship made of cheese,
Dreaming of snacks carried by the breeze.
With every wave, a laugh erupts,
As seagulls join in, fussing and cupped.

They sail past shores of jellybeans,
Where fortune's found in ice cream scenes.
Yet mishaps brew in every smile,
Spilling snacks! Oh, what a trial!

Shards of Skyborne Luck

I gathered stars in a bag so tight,
Hoping they'd grant me a wish tonight.
But one got out, flew right away,
And giggled, 'Catch me, if you may!'

The others danced just out of reach,
Playing tricks, like a rambunctious beach.
In my pursuit, I tumbled like stew,
Laughing too hard to feel so blue.

The Palette of Possibilities Above

In the sky, crayons soar and glide,
Painting clouds while the sun takes pride.
Each stroke a chance, a whimsy's call,
But oops! One fell—what a colorful fall!

Now rainbows dance with polka dots,
As glitter smiles in mischievous plots.
With laughter raining, the world spins round,
In this canvas of joy, luck is found.

Destiny's Colorful Cloak

A parrot with a top hat,
Swirls in unexpected noise,
He bets on a game of odds,
With a wink and rollicking poise.

A chicken joins the party,
Dressed in feathers bright and keen,
Together they plot their antics,
In a dance, a sight unseen.

The cards are shuffled wildly,
With luck's unpredictable flick,
The hen clucks out a giggle,
As the parrot plays a trick.

In this circus of blunders,
Laughter fills the sunny air,
For in the game of nonsense,
Who needs fortune when we dare?

Tailwinds of Triumph

A duck with dreams of flying,
Waddles forth with gleeful waddle,
He's got his eyes on the clouds,
Aerial feats are his throttle.

The seagull scoffs and cackles,
"Come down, you silly fowl!"
But the duck just quacks back laughter,
And puffs out his chest with a growl.

With a gust and a push of breeze,
He jumps and spirals about,
His flight's more like a belly flop,
But joy's what he's truly about.

As the sun sets on the sea,
His friends cheer in their delight,
For who won isn't what matters,
But the fun of the light-hearted flight.

Shimmering Aspirations Aloft

A cat in a tuxedo struts,
With visions of stardom bright,
He twirls with grace and swagger,
In the moon's soft silver light.

The mice below just chuckle,
With plans to steal all his cheese,
While the cat prances and poses,
As if his fame comes with ease.

His whiskers wiggle and dance,
In the spotlight, he plays king,
The mice sing an off-key tune,
To mock all his crazy bling.

In this oddball show of dreams,
Who's the fool, who's the star?
Maybe laughter's the true currency,
In this bizarre bazaar.

The Weightless Wealth of Wishes

A frog with a crown of bubbles,
Leaps with glee on lily pads,
He dreams of riches so silly,
In a land of soft, green rods.

A fly buzzes past him proudly,
Says, "I've got a thousand schemes!"
But the frog just grins and chuckles,
"Your fortune's just in your dreams!"

A dragonfly with shades appears,
Flashing wings in the sun's glow,
Who needs gold when you can dance?
In the brightest shows of flow?

So they leap and swirl together,
In the haze of twilight's hue,
For happiness is the treasure,
They find in the evening dew.

The Mystic Mix of Luck and Lift

If a chicken crossed the road,
Was it looking for a code?
To tap dance on the other side,
Or play poker for a ride?

Maybe it was feeling bold,
Dreaming of a pot of gold.
With every step it took in glee,
It thought, "Maybe it's just me!"

A duck quacked with a frown,
Watching feathers fall like crown.
"What's the secret, oh so grand?"
He just wished for a magic wand.

In a world so full of whim,
Where fortunes dance on every brim,
We laugh as luck plays hide and seek,
In silly games, we're all unique!

The Herald of Hidden Treasures

A parrot claims to know the way,
To treasures lost in bright cabaret.
With a beak that holds the master's clue,
He squawks, "Find me if you dare, it's true!"

A pirate with a wooden leg,
Keeps stumbling on a hidden keg.
"Is it riches or just stale rum?"
He wonders where the laughter's from.

Each map is scribbled in crayon bright,
Leading us to giggles of delight.
Why chase gold when giggles are near?
Let's trade our shovels for a beer!

So off we go, to a fanciful place,
With laughter lighting up our space.
Forget the treasures under the sand,
In funny moments, our luck expands!

Lattice of Leap and Livelihood

In a yard where puppies flee,
Doggy dreams of money trees.
Jumping high for tasty treats,
With each leap, he finds his feats.

A cat strolls by with nonchalance,
Wishing luck would match her dance.
She sways her tail like a diva queen,
Thinking of the gold sheen she's seen.

With every jump and every spin,
They chuckle at the hope within.
"Why work hard? Just play and laugh,
For joy's the best of all the crafts!"

They scheme together, a master plan,
A neighborhood feat they can't quite span.
But in the end, it's all for fun,
In liveliness, they've surely won!

Dreamcatcher's Aerial Embrace

A dreamcatcher spun in flight,
Hoping to catch joy tonight.
With laughter slipping through the yarn,
It caught a giggle from a barn.

Sheep were giggling in delight,
Finding humor in their plight.
What if they could spin and soar,
Every leap a chance for more?

As night descended, stars did wink,
Each twinkling light made them think.
"Let's catch happiness on the wing,
For that's the luck that makes us sing!"

So they tumbled through the air,
In whimsical dances, without a care.
For in the embrace of silly dreams,
They found the fortune of our themes!

Ethereal Threads of Goodness

In the sky, a bird prances,
Twirling dreams in feathered dances.
With each flap, a giggle flies,
Chasing fortunes in the skies.

Plucking smiles from clouds so bright,
They stitch joy in sheer delight.
Each stitch a laugh, each knot a cheer,
Who knew luck could tickle the ear?

The Magic Beneath the Air

Look closely, there's a playful breeze,
Wrapping secrets in the trees.
With silly whispers, it reveals,
The best of luck is what it steals.

A twisty turn, a windy chase,
Brings giggles in a funny race.
For every flap brings lots of mirth,
Who knew luck danced on the earth?

Shadows of Success in Softness

Down below, a shadow lurks,
Wearing charm in hidden quirks.
It prances lightly, spry and sly,
Collecting giggles as it flies.

With every flap, it stirs the air,
Scattering luck without a care.
A playful jolt, oh what a sight,
Success is buzzing with delight!

Ascending to Affluence

A whimsy bird climbs up the scale,
Its journey filled with laughter's trail.
Through thick and thin, it fluffs and struts,
Who knew success wore tiny nuts?

It drops a smile from way up high,
Sending giggles through the sky.
With each ascent, the fun expands,
Luck's a jester with soft hands!

Elysian Heights of Happening

In the realm where luck is a bird,
Chirping tales that seem absurd.
Juggling wishes in the air,
Like a clown without a care.

Sandwich of sand, a drink of rain,
Laughing at the frolic and pain.
Each twist of fate, a giggle spree,
While squirrels dance on a jubilee.

A cat in a hat, strutting around,
It sways with glee, never to frown.
Juggling jellybeans, oh what a sight,
As confetti bursts into the night.

With pickles in pockets and pies on our heads,
Chasing our dreams while avoiding the beds.
In a quirk-filled land of whimsical cheer,
Where laughter blooms with each passing year.

Threads of Triumph on High

In a loom made of laughter and glee,
We weave our fortunes like a decree.
With hiccups of joy and winks of delight,
Each thread that we pull brings new sights.

A squirrel with style, wearing a crown,
Dancing around in a whimsical gown.
Fortune favors those who can trip,
On banana peels, come join the flip!

Knotted in giggles, the fabric unfolds,
Stories of laughter, so silly, so bold.
We twirl through the skies, like kites in the breeze,
As luck tosses cookies, we munch with ease.

So bring on the blunders, we'll wear them with flair,
For every mishap is a reason to share.
In the tapestry bright, where humor aligns,
We find all our wealth in the punchlines we find.

The Glittering Lethe of Dreams

In a pool of chaos, we dive right in,
Chasing our hopes with a cheeky grin.
Doughnuts float by on a whimsical tide,
Where bubbles of laughter and joy coincide.

With rubbery chickens and socks on our heads,
We plot our adventures in mischief, not dread.
Forget about worries, let hilarity reign,
As we dance on the clouds in our own silly train.

While dreams wear sunglasses and roller skates,
We shuffle and shimmy, ignoring the fates.
Tickling the stars, we wiggle with jest,
In the land of mirth, we feel truly blessed.

So come take a plunge into giggly delight,
In the glittering depths where wrong turns are right.
We'll swim through the laughter and float through the beams,
Awash in the waves of our whimsical dreams.

Jovial Journeys in the Sky

With balloons and giggles, we sail on high,
Chasing the clouds, where the bunnies fly.
Kites of mischief and joy take a spin,
Where jokes are currency, let the fun begin!

Riding the rainbows, we prank the sun,
Sprinkling snickers on everyone.
A cat on a cloud, playing the flute,
And every note's a silly hoot.

Through twirls of cheer, we leap and bound,
With candy in hand, no worries around.
Adventure awaits at every twist and bend,
In the land of monkey business, where laughter won't end.

So grab a feather, let's take to the skies,
As we tickle the stars and bake pumpkin pies.
With a flourish of humor, our journey will gleam,
In the jovial land of our wildest dream.

The Aerial Gamble

With a toss of a bird on a sunny day,
A gamble was made in a silly way.
Hopes soared high as I flung a snack,
To see if fortune would find its track.

The pigeons danced in a feathery craze,
While I watched on in a daze ablaze.
One swooped down for a crumb or two,
And left me with nothing, just what to do!

A squirrel stepped in, with a cheeky flair,
Thinking he's clever, stealing my share.
But what's a bet on a sunny cheer?
As long as the birds come, I'll take my beer!

So here's to the skies, our laughter the prize,
In this game of chance, let the feathers rise.
For every misstep and each hasty chase,
There's joy in the moments, and nothing's a waste.

Woven Wishes

I crafted a dream out of threads and twine,
To weave my hopes like a grand design.
But every time I tossed it to the breeze,
It tangled itself with the neighbor's keys!

A cat took a liking, thought it a toy,
Chasing my visions with unfiltered joy.
I begged it to drop my finest work,
But it gave a leap, and I just went berserk!

At last, a lilting crow had its say,
Cawing a tune that led dreams astray.
Yet laughter erupted on that fateful day,
As wishes unraveled in silly dismay.

In the end, I found a blessing so near,
In chaos of threads—what was once fear.
These whimsical moments, how they do shine,
In every odd turn, fate draws a line.

Enchanted Drift

A balloon slipped away on a bright morning sky,
Leaving me grasping, with a half-hearted sigh.
It danced on the wind, like a bird on a spree,
I chased after laughter, caught nothing but glee!

With each twist and twirl, hopes took to flight,
It bobbed past the clouds, a wondrous sight.
Nearby, a kid laughed, released his own prize,
To join my balloon in aerial highs.

Two floaters collided, they wrangled and swirled,\nBouncing on breezes, their fates now unfurled.
What started as sorrow transformed to delight,\nAs balloons became buddies, a comical sight.

So here's to the drift, and to laughter we cling,
With each wayward whim, life's such a fling.
In the absurdity, treasures we find,
As joy takes its flight—oh, how we unwind!

The Silent Windfall

In the hush of the night, a whisper took flight,
With wishes that sparkled, to my sheer delight.
A squirrel in the tree, with his shifty little paws,
Held secrets of treasures with no visible cause.

I thought of plan schemes, from mischief to fun,
To capture the whispers before they were done.
But the nuts he collected, he shared with the moon,
While I watched in silence, feeling like a goon!

"Hey buddy!" I called, "What's your shifty scheme?"
But he just chattered back, like it was a dream.
Taking bets on a nut, or a dance with the stars,
In this wacky realm where I only had scars.

So here's to the winds that play tricks on the night,
Where fortune can hide in the soft, silly flight.
In laughter and folly, treasures are found,
Even in whispers where pets wear the crown.

Bright Pursuits in the Ether

A chicken once dreamed of a grand parade,
With glittering prizes and confetti made.
She fluffed up her wings, took a leap into air,
But landed in pie, with a plop and a flare.

Her friends cheered her on, hats askew with delight,
As she danced on the crust, oh what a sight!
"A winner in spirit!" the crowd did proclaim,
While she scratched at the crust, seeking fortune and fame.

A sly little fox, with a grin oh so wide,
Tried stealing the sparkles she wore with great pride.
But the chicken just giggled, then tickled his nose,
And off ran the fox, with no jewels to close.

So remember the chicken with dreams in the sky,
That fortune's not always where you think it lies.
Laugh with your heart, let your colors collide,
And dance through the mess, with your friends by your side.

Whimsy's Rise to Glory

A dandy old rooster, with tales to bestow,
Wore shades and a cape, and would strut to and fro.
He spoke of his dreams of a life full of cheer,
While rocking a beakful of fanciful gear.

The barnyard would giggle, in good-natured jest,
As he twirled and he foxtrotted—oh, what a quest!
"A feathered superstar!" the sheep all agreed,
While the goats took up notes in their barnyard creed.

Then one day came a cow, with a crown made of tin,
Proclaiming, "I'm queen! Now let the fun begin!"
But the dandy just laughed, fluffed his feathers with glee,
"I'll dance with my dreams, so come join me!"

So, in the spotlight, they boogied and swayed,
Creating a ruckus, in a grand masquerade.
A banquet of giggles, a feast fit for kings,
Whimsy found magic in the joy that it brings.

Tales of Gossamer and Glitter

A moth with grand plans, beneath the moonlight,
Thought he'd be a star, oh, what a sight!
He dressed up in sparkles, with glimmering glue,
And danced on a flower, in the morning dew.

But swatting flies came, not knowing his scheme,
Mistaking his moves for a comical dream.
"Just share the spotlight!" the moth hollered loud,
As he zipped past the bees, who buzzed in a cloud.

They chuckled and swirled, as the moth led the spree,
While the flowers applauded, "Let's party! Whee!"
Gossamer threads turned to glittering laughs,
Creating a story that the meadow now crafts.

So if you ever feel a bit lost in your flight,
Just pull on some sparkles and dance through the night.
For in the chaotic swirl of joy you'll find,
The tales that we share are simply divine.

The Bounty Beyond the Horizon

A squirrel with a vision, an acorn to chase,
Thought wealth was a nut hidden all in one place.
He climbed every tree, and he jumped from each peak,
With dreams of a stash that made others squeak.

He spotted a stash—oh, it sparkled and shone,
But it turned out to be just a shiny old cone.
"Not treasure, but laughter!" the squirrel then squealed,
As the forest all joined him, no more to conceal.

With friends all around, they rolled in the leaves,
Creating a fortune in giggles and heaves.
"Our bounty is found in the joy that we bring,
Not all of life's treasures are sealed with a ring!"

So follow the humor that dances like sun,
Life's riches are there, just waiting for fun.
Beyond every horizon, find giggles worldwide,
For fortune is laughter, in the sweet joy we ride.

Horizons of Elegance

A chicken in a tux, quite a sight,
Clucks and struts, a chic delight.
With bowtie askew and dance in his step,
He twirls through the barn, oh what a rep!

Pigs don their shades, lounging in style,
They sip on lemonade, pause for a while.
Bees buzz in polka dots, sweet and neat,
Planning a party on a velvet seat.

Ducks quack like pros, on the red carpet laid,
Waddling gracefully, unafraid.
While goats in top hats munch on fine cheese,
Chortling all day, with perfect ease.

When fashion meets farm, laughter takes flight,
In this quirky world, everything's right.
Dance like the dandy, fowl have their way,
In the land of good humor, come join the play!

Driftwood and Delights

On the shore, a crab clinks his shell,
With a wink and a nod, he casts a spell.
He found a driftwood, made of bright hues,
Said it's his treasure, for beauty and muse.

Seagulls wear hats, quite flamboyant and fine,
They gossip and giggle, sipping on brine.
The octopus, puzzled, tied up in knots,
Yells, 'Who needs eight arms when style's what you've got?'

An old sea turtle brings out his flair,
With shades on his eyes, he doesn't a care.
Crabs shuffle and dance, in fine sandy shoes,
As waves break in time, they sing their own blues.

Oh what a sight, the beach comes alive,
From driftwood to laughter, all creatures thrive.
With a twist and a turn, they all find a way,
To make every moment a tidal display!

The Lucky Quill

A silly bird sits, waddling in glee,
With a pen in her beak, and ideas set free.
She scratches and doodles on parchment so grand,
Her notes on foolishness, perfectly planned.

In the trees, there's a raccoon quite sly,
Wearing a vest, as he reaches for pie.
"Luck is just nonsense!" he boldly declared,
As he snitched all the treats that his friends had prepared.

Bouncing along, a hare hops in flair,
With a top hat adorned, and the silliest hair.
He proclaims his new rights to the best carrot patch,
While juggling a banana that nobody could catch!

All penned by the bird with the colorful quill,
Every line brings giggles and sees laughter spill.
In a world where mischief leads fortune to roam,
It's the lucky ones laughing that feel right at home!

Celestial Soirée

A star in a bow and a comet in dress,
Invite the whole universe, no need to impress.
Planets waltz gently, a rhythmic ballet,
As space dust and giggles blend into play.

The moon croons softly, a tune so divine,
While shooting stars bring snacks, the best of the line.
Galaxies giggle, with sparkle and cheer,
As they twirl and they spin with no hint of fear.

Asteroids clink glasses, toast to the night,
With laughter echoing, such a wondrous sight.
The cosmos in stitches as they float and glide,
In this grand soirée, where joy is the guide.

When twilight embraces, and all's said and done,
The universe winks, and the party's begun.
So gather your brilliance, let laughter ignite,
In this stellar adventure, all wrongs turn to right!

The Golden Quarantine

In a house of glittery gold,
A chicken turned rich, or so I'm told.
He gobbled up coins and danced all day,
While the neighbors just watched in dismay.

His feathers were bright, the envy of all,
But when he'd strut, he'd trip and fall.
Pigeon pals laughed at his clumsy show,
"Who knew wealth could make you so slow?"

One day he flew, with glint in his eye,
Over the fence, aiming for the sky.
Yet a napping dog gave a surprising shock,
And he landed in mud, what a laughable block!

Now he's a star in his little domain,
A golden fool with a silly fame.
With shiny dreams and lopsided flair,
He's the silliest bird, and he doesn't care!

The Beach of Chances

On a shore where the seagulls squawk,
A crab found a pearl, just taking a walk.
He donned a crown made of seashells wide,
As waves crashed, he'd dance with pride.

A flounder swam by, eyeing it all,
"Where'd you get that bling? You've made quite a haul!"
But each time he winked, he got sand in his eye,
'Fun is short when you're royal and shy!'

The fish threw a party, with snacks on display,
Yet the crab spent the night losing pearls in the fray.
While diving for treasure, he tripped on a rock,
Now he's the king, but can't quite walk!

As tides ebb and flow with a giggling cheer,
He reigns on the beach, with no hint of fear.
In his shell-tastic crown, he's quite the delight,
A crab with a dream, making wrongs turn to right.

Wings of Whimsy

A bird with style, in a hat too grand,
Took to the skies, with a band of sand.
They swirled and twirled, oh what a display,
Doing the cha-cha in a dainty ballet.

The wind blew strong, tossed them around,
With feathers flying like leaves off the ground.
The leader took flight, a bit out of line,
Landed in pie—what a silly design!

Yet down in the grove, a party soon brewed,
With baked goods aplenty, and fun's been renewed.
One pecked at frosting, the other stole treats,
Making a mess of their feathery feats.

In mismatched tuxedos, they danced through the night,
Under the stars, feeling oh-so-right.
With giggles and chuckles, what a sight to behold,
These winged party-goers, champions of bold!

Plumes of Prosperity

In a village where plumage was green,
Lived a duck with a dream, a quirky zest unseen.
He fancied himself a millionaire,
Though his pond was muddy and his feathers rare.

He planned to invest in a cornucopia,
But all he bought was silly utopia.
With pockets of glitter and bubblegum sheen,
He strutted around like a feathered machine.

The townsfolk chuckled at his grand schemes,
While he plotted for riches that danced in his dreams.
But each time he flapped, he'd lose a bright bill,
Yet he quacked with laughter, insisting, "What thrill!"

In the end, he found charm, not a fortune indeed,
With laughter and friends, he was wealthy, agreed.
For every odd moment turned gold in his heart,
In a world full of whimsy, he'd mastered the art!

A Caress from Above

A bird drops a penny from high in the sky,
I laugh as it clangs, oh my, oh my!
With every flapping wing, a coin's flight,
Perhaps I'm the chosen, what a delight!

A swaggering crow in a top hat does strut,
Picking through crumbs, it looks rather cut.
With a wink and a nod, it shows me the way,
To riches aplenty, or so they say!

I tossed out a sandwich, not caring to share,
Yet the winged gentleman's charm fills the air.
"Step right up, folks, and don't be shy!"
As we dance to the song of a bird-baked pie!

So next time you hear a chirp from a crow,
Remember the tales that the birds might bestow.
For who knows what secrets the skies might convey,
With feathers of laughter, oh joyful display!

The Aviary of Gold

In a park where the sparrows all sing with flair,
One swings on a branch, adjusting its hair.
With glittery wings, it calls out a tune,
As butterflies gather 'neath a bright balloon.

A duck in a tux, oh what a grand sight,
Quacking with style from morning till night.
It tips its fine hat to all walking by,
"Invest in the pond, the profits are high!"

A parrot with style, has wisdom to share,
"Don't put all your eggs in one basket, beware!"
With a wink and a squawk, it shares worldly truths,
Who knew that the birds were such fantastical sleuths?

So when you are out, and the avian crew,
Dresses in finery, just look at their view.
For amid the feathers, both silly and bold,
Lies a treasure of laughter far richer than gold!

Secrets in the Breeze

A robin once whispered a secret to me,
About a lost fortune beneath the old tree.
I followed its trail, till I tripped on a stone,
And rolled down a hill, but I laughed on my own.

With each gust of wind, new riddles unfold,
A seagull, quite cheeky, speaks tales to be told.
It flaps its wide wings, showing off quite a lot,
As I pondered, "Is this the best deal I've got?"

An owl in a scarf starts to chuckle and sway,
"Don't worry, dear human, you'll find your own way!
The true prize is joy, wrapped up in a riddle,
So dance with the whims, there's no time to whittle!"

As I gathered my wits, ready to fly,
The birds laughed together, keeping birds-eye high.
Their secrets now blend with the breeze in the air,
A reminder that laughter is found everywhere!

The Feathered Talisman

A quirky old bird tried to sell me some charms,
With feathers and sparkles, it waved its short arms.
"Just rub it for luck!" it cawed with delight,
While pecking my shoe, what a curious sight!

A pigeon with swagger pulled cash from its sock,
"Join my club now, or feel the real shock!"
I laughed at the antics of this feathery crook,
As it shuffled its feet, quite the sight to look.

With avian tricks and some sleight of the wing,
This troupe of clowns found new ways to bling.
From jesters in feathers to dapper old crows,
They turned mundane days into grand circus shows!

So if ever you stumble on birds with a flair,
Join their feathered party, don't just stand and stare!
For treasures of laughter they carry with grace,
In a talisman of fun, there's always a place!

The Soft Touch of Serendipity

Once a chicken found a dime,
She danced around, oh so sublime.
Clucking tunes of joy and glee,
A wealth of giggles, can't you see?

A pair of socks, green and bright,
Gave a pigeon quite a fright.
He strutted proud, in garish flair,
Winning hearts with feathers rare.

A lucky hat, three sizes too wide,
Brought smiles and laughter, no need to hide.
With every flap, a quirk and twist,
In fortune's game, how could you resist?

So here's to luck on a silly spree,
Mixing colors and comedy.
In every slip and clumsy dance,
Lies a nugget of sweet romance.

Sails of Silk and Secrets

A cat in a boat, oh what a sight,
With sails that glittered in the moonlight.
He searched for fish, but found a hat,
A treasure trove of quirk, imagine that!

A raccoon stole the goldfish bowl,
With a pirate's swagger, he took control.
In the midst of splashes and a loud cheer,
He declared himself the captain here.

The wind whispered tales of laughs untold,
Of monkeys in velvet, so daring and bold.
With every lurch, the boat would sway,
Each secret cry led them astray.

So set your sails on mischief's breeze,
For laughter and whimsy are sure to please.
In a world where misfits cleverly scheme,
You'll find the magic in a glorious dream.

Whispers of Wealth on the Wind

A squirrel found nuts, he thought he was rich,
Enticed by a fortune, without a hitch.
But his stash attracted a hungry bear,
"More nuts!" he cried, "please do beware!"

A crow with a jewel, bright as the sun,
Decided to trade for a crumbling bun.
"Oh, what a deal!" the crumbs went flying,
As he cawed and strutted, the whole tree sighing.

The breeze carried giggles from tree to tree,
Where critters shared secrets and sips of tea.
Wealth isn't gold, but laughter, they say,
A treasure of jokes to brighten the day.

So gather your friends, let's share the fun,
In a world where laughter has just begun.
With whispers of joy swaying through our minds,
We'll find our riches, no need for kinds.

Clouds of Chance

A parrot spun tales of improbable dreams,
While clouds drifted by, bursting at the seams.
"Let's fly to the moon, ride raindrops with glee!"
Though landing on stars felt a bit tricky.

An owl with glasses made quite the fuss,
Forecasting fun without any rush.
He calculated giggles, a recipe bright,
Capping the whimsy beneath the starlight.

A rabbit in overalls planned a grand show,
With acrobatic flips, giving everyone woe.
"Watch carefully now, it's all part of my dance!
Don't get distracted by sweet, clumsy chance!"

With every sigh and a playful cheer,
The clouds whispered joy, so close and near.
In every cloud that drifts and twirls,
Hide dilly-dally dreams and frolicsome pearls.

Breeze-Borne Bounties

A chicken once dreamed of flight,
She flapped her wings with all her might.
But when she soared above the ground,
Her lunch fell out, oh what a sound!

With popcorn scattered all around,
The pigeons laughed, they gathered 'round.
"You think you're slick, but we know better,"
As she chased crumbs in a great big sweater.

Her dreams of soaring in the sky,
Quickly turned to wondering why.
The breeze was fun, the view was grand,
But lunch was lost, it slipped her hand!

So now she struts with fashion flair,
A chicken queen beyond compare.
In sparkling hats and shoes so bright,
She's found her fortune in funny flight!

The Harmonious Ascension

A penguin tried to take a dive,
In hopes to fly, oh how they strive!
He flapped his flippers, gave a cheer,
But missed the wind, and drank a beer!

His buddies chuckled as he fell,
"You're a bird, but not so swell!"
With each attempt, the laughter grew,
They formed a band, and off they flew!

They crooned a tune on icy hills,
While he still dreamt of soaring thrills.
Their harmonies rose like a kite,
But he just waddled with delight.

So now he dances when they sing,
He may not fly, but what a king!
For fortune's found in laughter shared,
Where even penguins feel prepared!

Cherished Chimes of the Cloud

A sparrow stole a silver spoon,
And thought he'd dine beneath the moon.
He set a table on a cloud,
Inviting friends, he felt so proud!

But when the first course took a nosedive,
His new cuisine didn't quite survive.
The soup was soup-er, but the toast took flight,
And all his guests vanished from sight!

He chased after donuts through the air,
While giggles filled the cool night air.
With pies and tarts, they played a game,
Of which one would be the spoon's true flame?

Now every night, they host a feast,
In the clouds, where laughers convene at least.
A banquet of joy, a flighty parade,
Where every mishap is a splendid charade!

Dreamy Motifs on a Feather's Edge

A peacock pranced with colors bright,
He dreamt of fame under the starlight.
"To strut my stuff, I must look grand!"
Said he while plotting in the sand.

With sequins lined upon his tail,
He danced and wiggled, never pale.
But tripped on his own glossy plume,
And tumbled down into a bloom!

His friends all gasped, then laughed out loud,
As he arose, a flowery shroud.
"A garden throne!" he claimed with grace,
And flowered hats—he found his place!

Now every show, it's all the rage,
To fall and rise onto the stage.
For glory lies in laughter's bridge,
In the best of times, take a funny ridge!

Whispers of the Sky

In the air, a bird doth strut,
Wearing shoes too big, but what the nut!
It tried to dance and twirl about,
But landed flat, oh what a pout!

The clouds giggled, they couldn't hide,
As the bird slipped, oh what a ride!
With wings so bright and heart so bold,
It thought it was worth its weight in gold!

A breeze gave a laugh, swift as can be,
Pulled its tail, oh, let it be free!
Down came the feathers, a fluttery mess,
"I'm simply too grand for all this stress!"

But still, the bird, it shook and danced,
With moves so quirky, it had us entranced!
And up in the sky, laughter rang clear,
For a silly little bird, we'd all cheer!

Wings of Prosperity

A chicken strutted in a top hat,
Claimed it was hip, oh what of that?
With a waddle, it preened and posed,
Boasting tales, oh how it glows!

It found some worms and then it thought,
"I'm the richest bird that ever was taught!"
But slipped in mud and went splat!
Now that's one way to lose a hat!

Gathering friends for a feast divine,
They brought out seeds and drank some wine.
"Who needs treasure when fun's at play?
We'll have a party every day!"

As the moon rose, they danced in glee,
The richest of birds were they, you see!
With every squawk and silly little peep,
They found their fortune, their hearts to keep!

The Gilded Plume

A peacock roamed with a thriving air,
Wore a golden crown, quite a flair!
Strutting around, a sight to behold,
Yet tripped on its tail, oh the bold!

It puffed up proud, flared out its wings,
But then got distracted by shiny things.
A glittery rock, it just couldn't resist,
And let out a squawk, "Oh, that's on my list!"

It scooped up sparkles, plumes all aglow,
"Look at me shine, come on, let's go!"
But as it leapt, it stumbled around,
And rolled in the mud, now what a sound!

Yet through all the tumbles and silly digs,
It stood there laughing, oh how it jigs!
For riches are fun, but oh, what a mess,
A life filled with laughs is truly the best!

A Dance of Luck

A tiny sparrow with a bright green hat,
Dreamed of riches as it sat!
It practiced moves all day and night,
Hoping to dance into fortune's light!

With a wiggle and jig, it swirled with glee,
In front of a mirror, "Look at me!"
But a gust of wind came out of nowhere,
And flipped it around, oh that poor dear!

It landed right in a pool of pies,
Eyes wide opened with surprise!
Sticky fingers and a berry stain,
"Oh look," it chirped, "I'm a dessert train!"

But soon all the friends began to gather,
For a pie party that made them all chatter.
In the mess, they found what they lacked,
Joyful hearts, and that's a fact!

Plumage of Promise

A parrot taught to dance, oh what a sight,
With sequined wings that shimmer bright.
He struts with flair, a plucky parade,
His jokes about pirates? Never invade!

The pigeons gossip, they can't get enough,
Of his tales of treasures, silly yet tough.
In the park, he's the king of the chat,
While squirrels roll their eyes, just look at that!

But one day he tripped, on a mat made of cheese,
His graceful performance brought all to their knees.
With a squawk and a tumble, the laughter was grand,
A hero, he flew, though not quite as planned!

Yet still every evening, he winks as he flies,
Telling tall tales that bewilder the wise.
With a heart full of giggles, our bird takes his bow,
In plumage of promise, oh what a wow!

Serendipity's Soft Caress

A goose with a hat, as fanciful as can be,
Pranced down the lane, full of jubilee.
His feathers all fluffed, he strutted with pride,
Spreading joy and laughter with every wide stride.

The townsfolk all chuckled, they gathered around,
As he quacked witty rhymes that astound.
He'd spread out his wings, a grand, feathered show,
While squirrels took notes, their fans in tow.

Then one fateful day, he sat on a pie,
The crust gave a squish, oh my, oh me, oh my!
With whipped cream attire and a laugh in the air,
He left such a mess, yet none seemed to care.

In the end, he soared into stories untold,
With each silly mishap, his legend grew bold.
A soothing reminder, life's best when you jest,
Each quack brings a cheer, making every heart blessed.

Woven Tales of Aerial Grace

A robin who loved to weave hats out of twine,
Crafted a topper that sparkled and shined.
He'd wear it to tea with the doves and the crows,
While sharing great tales of his flapping woes.

One day, he discovered a very fine sock,
And turned it to fashion, all the rage around the block.
With silky designs and a patch here and there,
He flaunted his style with incomparable flair.

The sparrows rolled in laughter, they couldn't believe,
A bird in a sock? It was hard to conceive!
But our robin just winked, in his cozy attire,
With feathers all fluffed, he shone like a fire.

Now festivals bloom, where hats fly on high,
A runway of laughs as the hours drift by.
His whimsy ignites all who gather and cheer,
In woven tales of joy that wrap us so near.

The Golden Harvest of Skybound Dreams

A finch with ambition, a songbird with flair,
Sought out the best of the sky's golden air.
He chased shiny wishes like fireflies at night,
Hoping to catch one, oh what a delight!

But when he went fishing for stars in the blue,
He hooked a bright comet, just zipping on through!
With splashes of glitter and shimmers of light,
He squealed in pure joy—what a glorious sight!

In his beak he held dreams, unshaped and untamed,
He giggled at plans he had never yet named.
Now dancing on daisies, he leads the parade,
With shenanigans, laughter, a grand masquerade.

But oh, what a tease, one dream slipped away,
Chased by a breeze over hills made of hay.
Yet still he keeps flying, with tunes full of glee,
In the golden harvest of whimsy, you see!

The Flutter of Fortuity

In a world of chance and mishap,
A chicken crossed the road, oh snap!
With a strut so bold and a quirky dance,
It tripped on dreams, took a wild chance.

A squirrel with pockets, so stuffed with nuts,
Said, "Go for broke! Just push your luck!"
While butterflies laugh with a tickled breeze,
They flutter by in a hilarious tease.

Jokers flip coins without a care,
Luck's a jester who's never fair.
In a whimsical whirl, they spin and twirl,
This wild ride's a glorious swirl!

So if you're feeling lost and blue,
Just laugh out loud; that will do!
For in this game of twists and turns,
The best of luck is what one earns!

Twisted Trails of Dauntless Dreams

Once a dreaming hedgehog braved the night,
With a top hat on, quite a funny sight.
In a forest rave, he wiggled and shook,
Spinning tales in every nook!

A rabbit named Gus had grand plans too,
To dance like a fool and chase a shoe.
But on his quick hop, he slipped on a sprout,
And rolled down the hill with an uproarious shout!

They say the owls hoot with wise old tricks,
But join the party for some laughs and licks!
As moonbeams twinkle and shadows sway,
Fortune's feeling rather fray.

Through tangled paths and dandelion dreams,
Adventure springs forth in giggles and beams.
So chase those trails, not fears, you see,
For joy will guide you, wild and free!

Softly Delivered Serendipity

In a cloud of giggles, a postman flies,
Delivering joy with feathery sighs.
He stumbles and tumbles, oh what a sight!
His cart filled with laughter, pure delight!

A penguin in pajamas, lounging with flair,
Ordered a pizza—it's quite unfair!
With toppings of jelly and chocolate sweet,
He served it up slick on a lovely sheet!

In the café of whims, a fish in a hat,
Claims fortune swims where the giggles are at.
So raise your juice boxes, toast to the bends,
For luck's a wild friend that never quite ends!

With letters of joy, and sassy wit,
Each moment's a gift—don't just sit!
So stretch your arms wide and hug the day,
For surprises abound in a silly ballet!

Beneath the Wings of Wealth

A parrot on a perch said, "Life's a ball!"
With bling on his beak, he's got it all!
He squawked about riches in the finest style,
While squirrels debated their nutty pile.

In a pocket of dreams, a snail drew a map,
Said "Follow my trail, avoid the gap!"
But tripped on a toadstool, oh what a fall,
Laughter erupted, and that was the call!

The rabbits were racing in velvet and lace,
In a whirl of confetti, they picked up the pace.
The key to abundance isn't just gold,
It's sharing some chuckles and being bold!

So under the sky, with hearts opened wide,
Celebrate the silly and take it in stride.
For beneath those wings, wherever they veer,
Fortune is frolicking, let's spread some cheer!

The Flight of Fickle Fate

A chicken crosses, what a plight,
To dodge the cars on a moonlit night.
Who knew a leap could lead to fame,
Or end up in a viral game?

The squirrel's stash, it flies away,
A gust of breeze on a sunny day.
He chases dreams in nutty flurries,
While passersby just giggle in worries.

A clumsy cat with wings so bright,
Attempts to soar with all its might.
But it flops down, a fluffy mess,
The purring laughter, we can't suppress.

In whimsy's hold, we find delight,
For life's absurdities take to flight.
Each twist and turn, a giggling twist,
In this dance of chance, we can't resist.

Celestial Blessings in the Breeze

A seagull swoops, a snack in tow,
Impeccable aim, don't you know?
It snatches fries from a toddler's hand,
The laughter rings across the strand.

A paper plane takes off with glee,
Flies over heads like it's fancy-free.
But turns around, much to our shock,
And lands right on an old man's sock!

The wind decided it's prankster born,
Sending hats to places forlorn.
We chase them down, a joyful race,
While giggling hard, we lose our place.

Oh, life's a breeze of silly sights,
A festival of clumsy flights.
With laughter leading, we'll pretend,
This whimsy's magic never ends.

Wind-Swept Musings of the Heart

The breeze brings whispers, oh so rare,
Of kites that dance without a care.
But when the wind takes off with grace,
It leaves behind a shoe or lace.

A butterfly laughs at a dancing leaf,
While a dog dreams big, believing its chief.
Yet in pursuit of joy and fun,
It trips on branches, oh what a run!

Rain clouds chuckle, lightning winks,
As puddles fill in whimsical links.
Jumping high, we splash with pride,
In nature's antics, we now abide.

Our hearts take wing with silly plans,
To chase the clouds and join their dance.
For in this world of whims and jest,
We find true joy, we feel the best.

Ascendance in the Airwaves

A simple kite, a string unspooled,
In a tangled flight, it looks quite fooled.
It sails away on a wild spin,
While onlookers laugh, 'Is that a win?'

A rubber ducky, up so high,
Takes to the wind, what a bold goodbye!
But with a squawk, it falls with glee,
Bouncing back, oh would you believe?

The cat on a broom, oh what a sight,
It zooms through the air in sheer delight.
But then trips over its own long tail,
As the laughter erupts, it sets to wail.

In the airwaves twirl the whims of fate,
With every misstep, we celebrate.
In laughter's embrace, we find our cheer,
In this crazy world, we're happy here.

The Plumage Prophecy

A parrot with dreams of gold,
Said, "Hey, will I be rich when I'm old?"
The canary laughed and danced with glee,
"You're plucking coins? Just stick with me!"

The rooster crowed, "I'll have my say,
I'm saving for a fancy café!"
But he only served bugs and mud pie stew,
Who knew breakfast could taste so askew?

A peacock strutted, feathers a-show,
Claiming, "I'm the star of the show!"
But his fans were just flies buzzing near,
"Your tail's a mess, my friend, oh dear!"

So feathers could dream, but fortunes were slim,
In a barn where jokes met a whimsical whim!
Life may be funny, with riches unplanned,
The best luck could be in a comical band!

The Soaring Aspirant

A duckling decided, "I'll fly to the moon,
With swagger and style, I'll arrive there soon!"
He crafted a rocket from leaves and a pot,
But forgot that his kin liked the pond a lot.

His friends quacked loudly, "You can't leave us here!
We'll miss your jokes and your wobbly cheer!"
But he flapped his wings and he gave it a go,
With hopes of a flight show, like no one could know.

Yet when he took off, he soared with a quack,
And landed right in a neighbor's snack!
"I've touched the stars!" he proudly proclaimed,
While munching on crumbs, oddly unashamed.

So the lesson was clear, for all birds to see,
Adventure can lead you right back to the brie!
A fortune of crumbs and a laugh-filled flight,
From one wobbly duck who took on the night!

Beneath the Starlit Wing

A sparrow once chirped under stars so bright,
"Do you think I can dance?" oh what a sight!
With a flurry of twirls and a flap of delight,
She tripped on her toe, but said, "That's all right!"

The owls hooted softly, their heads in a spin,
"At least you're not stuck with a feathered fin!"
They rolled on the branches, all chuckles galore,
As the sparrow kept dancing, vowing for more.

While the moon softly winked, peeking down low,
The night filled with laughter and warm, gentle glow.
With each clumsy step, she embodied pure cheer,
In the heart of the night, beneath starlit veneer.

"Who needs a partner when I've got my flair?
I can twirl with the breeze, and float through the air!"
The lesson so clear, beneath night's soft swing,
It's laughter and joy that can make your heart sing!

Mysteries in the Air

Up high where the clouds were as fluffy as pie,
A detective bird asked, "Who could deny?"
With a magnifying glass and a cap on his head,
He searched for lost treasures in stories long dead.

The doves cooed softly, "What's that you pursue?
A piece of old cheese, or a shoe?"
The hawk flew by, with a chuckle and scoff,
"I found a stray sandwich, come take a bite off!"

The mystery deepened, as crumbs hit the ground,
"Where's the hidden fortune? It feels lost, not found!"
The gulls made a ruckus, with jest and with cheer,
"Perhaps it's the laughter that brings fortune near!"

So this bird detective, with his friends on the run,
Discovered that fun was the ultimate fun!
The mysteries shared, in the fresh morning air,
Were treasures of joy, that they'd always declare!

Echoes of Abundance

A chicken crossed the road to boast,
In dreams of grain, she is the host.
She strutted proud with a cluck and cheer,
While ducks rolled their eyes in the mirror near.

Her feathers were gold, or so she claimed,
As she danced around, never quite tamed.
With every step, she kicked up the dust,
And the barnyard whispered, 'In her we trust!'

The cow rolled her eyes, munching on hay,
'Seriously, what's a chicken's day?'
But the rooster crowed loud, 'Join in the fun!'
As they all laughed under the setting sun.

So if you're feeling down, take a clue,
Pretend you're a bird, fly high and true.
For laughter's the grain that feeds the soul,
In this silly barn, we all play a role.

The High-Flying Muse

A parrot once wanted to write a book,
About all the nonsense that crazy birds cook.
She perched on a branch with a grand, vivid pen,
And squawked, 'I'll be famous! Just wait 'til then!'

But the sparrows just giggled, 'What a funny sight!'
With her tales of mischief, day turned to night.
She scribbled on leaves, but forgot her rhymes,
While owls blinked slowly, counting the chimes.

The peacock strutted, full of himself,
Said, 'I'm more stunning than any book's shelf!'
But the parrot winked, 'Your beauty's so bright,
With you in my stories, we'll take flight tonight!'

Birds gathered 'round, sharing laughs and glee,
As tales in the wind danced wild and free.
So raise up your voices, let funny tales bloom,
And chase all your dreams—there's always room!

Threads of Fate

A rabbit once spun a thread of luck,
With bits of mischief and a sprinkle of pluck.
She wove and she wobbled, a curious sight,
While all of her friends gathered in delight.

'Is that silk or just fluff?' the wise old cat asked,
With a twitch of his tail, he was clearly tasked.
'These threads hold the laughter, the giggles we share,
Life's full of surprises, if you just dare!'

A turtle piped up, slow but astute,
'Wrap me in fortune; I'd love a new suit!'
As the rabbit spun faster, her laugh was a song,
Transforming her friends, where they all belong.

So, stitch your own stories with colorful cheer,
Life's a grand quilt if you hold it near.
With humor as fabric and smiles interlaced,
You'll find that your path is eternally graced.

Ribbons in the Wind

A kite flew high, pulling laughter down,
As kids chased joy across the town.
With ribbons streaming and tails in the breeze,
They danced in the sky with the greatest of ease.

The winds whispered secrets, coaxing them near,
'Take a chance on a whim, there's nothing to fear!'
A gust of absurdity swept through the park,
And the kite took off with a flamboyant spark.

If life is a string, let it twist and twine,
Laugh at the knots, let your spirit shine.
For in every flutter, there's magic unfurled,
As the ribbons in wind write a tale of the world.

Harmony in the High Heavens

In skies where dreams might frolic,
Clouds wear coats, all bumpy and symbolic.
Pigeons dance with swanky-like flair,
While squirrels jump, without a care.

A kite with style, like a fancy hat,
Zooms in circles, how about that?
They laugh at gravity, a silly pact,
While landing poorly, a comical act.

Stars twinkle brightly, oh what a jest,
Wishing on wishes, put to the test.
A cat in a rocket, sipping tea,
Looks at the moon, and shouts, "Whee!"

So here's to the laughter above our heads,
Where luck is found, and joy spreads.
In this high place, life's a fun chase,
With each giggle, we leave a trace.

Glimmers in the Gossamer

A spider spins dreams, winks with delight,
Webs like jewels, catching moonlight.
Flies crash landing, such hapless fliers,
While ants in suits earn their tiny hire.

Buzzing bees throw disco balls,
On flower dance floors, they twirl and sprawl.
Pollen confetti in a golden cheer,
They hum a tune we all like to hear.

Butterflies wear capes, on the loose,
In the garden, they cut quite the truce.
Chasing sunbeams in a wild chase,
Wings ablaze, in a colorful race.

Among the glimmers, laughter flows,
With every flutter, the whimsy grows.
In this silly realm, let worries cease,
As joy and giggles dance with ease.

The Rapture of Rising Winds

The gales come racing, what a sight,
They twist and swirl, full of delight.
Kites take flight in a zigzag spree,
While hats get thrown in a gusty glee.

Trees sway gently, a playful tease,
Whispering secrets with the breeze.
Puppies chasing leaves in a whirl,
While cats look on, with a bored curl.

A windy day, the jokes fall fast,
As clouds float by, some shapes are cast.
A dinosaur here, a fishy friend,
With every gust, it's laughter they send.

So raise a toast to the airy bloom,
Where silliness reigns, banishing gloom.
With every puff, let joy ascend,
In swirling spirals, our spirits mend.

Beneath the Canopy of Hopes

Beneath the trees, where giggles grow,
Squirrels play poker, in sun's warm glow.
Bunnies bet carrots, a floppy disguise,
While owls judge games with their wise, round eyes.

Dancing shadows in a leafy dance,
Make the sunbeam take a chance.
They twist and jive, what a show,
With each little stomp, their joy will flow.

Under this roof, the fun won't cease,
Every rustling leaf shouts, "Release!"
The squirrels leap, oh what a sight,
Chasing dreams in the gentle twilight.

So gather round, where laughter lies,
In the heart of fun, where magic flies.
Beneath these branches, we pose and play,
With every chuckle, we brighten the day.

www.ingramcontent.com/pod-product-compliance
Lightning Source LLC
Chambersburg PA
CBHW070008300426
43661CB00141B/445